Vegan Meal Plan

Authentic Asian Recipes

Adrianna F. Piper

Contents

Chapter One

ASIAN FAVORITES MADE EASY

From

From sweet and sour sautés to creamy Massaman curries, Vietnamese new summer rolls, and Chinese Bao buns, this cookbook celebrates the flavors of the East and demonstrates how easy it is to design unique and delicious vegetarian dinners in your own particular kitchen, even on the busiest weeknights.

The Ultimate Asian Cookbook for Vegans brings together vibrant cuisine from Thailand to Malaysia to Japan, demonstrating that even the most inexperienced chef can easily recreate authentic meals at home. Every recipe has been tried, tested, and developed to hold the sensitive types of the East, with a few tweaks to make it vegetarian-friendly.

The Love Vegan cookbook series is based on the idea that delicious, energizing, and really upgraded cuisine may be produced using basic, easy-to-find ingredients. Weeknight suppers should take no more than 30 minutes to prepare, and will provide you and your family with meals that rival take-out.

This cookbook series aims to provide some insight into the vegetable loving lifestyle as well as the health benefits that come with it. We believe that whatever your motivations for including vegetarian cuisine into your diet, the end result should be flavorful and trustworthy. Whether you're a vegetarian lover, a vegan, or a meat eater looking to reduce the amount of meat-based dinners in your diet, this book may help you stay motivated to create delicious meals throughout the week.

So what are you waiting for? Start your Asian vegetarian journey now!

Go straight to the recipes.

Chapter Two

VEGANISM IN A NUTSHELL

Veganism\shas generally been considered to be an extreme dietary lifestyle, yet an ever increasing number of\sindividuals are moving towards eating not so much meat but rather more plant-based food. The need to carry on with a sound way of life in this day and age is undeniable. Like never before we are confronted with expanded pressure that subverts our body's safe frameworks, also the numerous synthetic substances, chemicals and poisons we are exposed to through our food consumption. It subsequently checks out to expand the amount of regular and effectively absorbable food varieties in our eating regimen to give our body the most obvious opportunity we jar of being better and thriving.

The normal meat-eater devours multiple times more every day protein than their bodies need. You can get the essential every day protein from a delectable dish like Quinoa, Avocado and Spinach Sushi Rolls. Add a crawl of salted ginger and a touch of wasabi and you take care of your protein, omega oil and iron admission for the afternoon. Ginger gives you an incredible stomach related and safe framework lift and wasabi is loaded with hostile to disease benefits as well as arousing your taste buds with its sharp chomp. What a solid and flavorful option in contrast to a sleek burger and fries!

Why add vegetarian food to your eating routine? Western civilisation consumes significantly more meat than Eastern civilisations, and we are undeniably less smart for it. Development chemicals in milk and meat are added to build the development cycle, and when eaten, these chemicals and unnatural substances are moved to your body and cause devastation and change to qualities. This makes numerous undesirable clinical ailments like untimely pubescence, asthma and stomach related messes which can all be kept away from by following a superior eating plan. Everything necessary is essentially adding more vegetables, entire grains and heartbeats to your eating routine, and this cookbook can help by motivating you to cook inventive and invigorating plans. The more normal fixings you eat, the more you are pursuing a superior and better you.

So what is a vegetarian? There is a distinction in the eating routine of veggie lovers and vegetarians. Genuine veganism is a dietary way of life where no creature items are consumed by any stretch of the imagination. It isn't just with regards to the food they eat yet additionally the ecological effect and the longing to lessen the tension on the earth's\sresources.

Vegans are aware of the carbon impression of the food they devour. They endeavor to guarantee the effect is just about as insignificant as could be expected. Albeit genuine veganism is taking out all creature items from your eating routine, we accept you ought to do what works for you. Vegetarians, then again won 't drink any meat, however they will eat creature produce like eggs, cheddar and milk. As there are such countless secret creature items in food, a veggie lover or vegan must be exceptionally cautious with what they eat. Would it be a good idea for you need to go without meat make certain to peruse the fixings on items, do a touch of examination and consistently pose inquiries in eateries. You'd be shocked to observe that numerous a vegetable soup has been made with chicken stock!

So many individuals avoid veganism since they don 't really accept that an unadulterated plant based diet can fulfill their taste buds, yet this couldn't possibly be more off-base. They have this picture of vegetarians either being Buddhist priests or hipsters. While both of these are way of life decisions and both have extremely sound standards, they may not be the most ideal way for you to go. Our grandmas with their dim broccoli that used to leave a watery wreck on our plates are a long ways from a new, fresh pan fried food or a delicious Pad

Thai that you will find in this cookbook. Veganism is thinking outside about the case, it is an alternate perspective on and at life. This book will toss that picture of dim broccoli out of the window everlastingly and demonstrate that real heavenly food can be accessible for the vegetarian diet too.

Most of us can verify being totally frustrated by plans that case to be absolutely veggie lover, just for them to highlight some 'covered up' creature items or taste like crude tofu. Each recipe in this book has been carefully tried, tested and refined to retain an authentic flavor and best of all, each recipe is not only suitable for vegans but also for people who desires to make their eating habits healthier and tastier.

You can substitute the spices, flavors or some other fixings utilized in our plans to add your unique touch. The significant thing to recollect is that the best culinary specialists cook with their heart. They explore different avenues regarding food. Be trying, be imaginative and utilize these plans as a base for making new plans of\syour own. Use them as a springboard into an intriguing universe of vegetarian cooking and you will not be disappointed.

Go straight to the recipe section.

PLANT BASED POWER\s'You are what you eat'

The expanding fame of the veggie lover diet is connected to a developing number of critical and very much archived medical advantages.

As of late, the\smedia has revealed some insight into the plant-based way of life and suppressed any legends that a veggie lover diet can't adequately source every one of the supplements we really want to carry on with a solid and healthy lifestyle. There is plenty of science to support a plant based diet but personal transformations such as curing diabetes, overcoming obesity and leading a more active and energized life seem to make the biggest impression.

Whether you choose to cause one day seven days a meatless day or regardless of whether you to choose to completely take on a vegetarian way of life you will feel much improved, have more energy and be more impervious to disease. It is vital to remember that what you put into your body should be working with your body, not against it. It is a similar idea as running uphill rather than running along a level way. More energy is exhausted by processing meat and handled food than by eating effectively edible and nutritious vegetables and pulses.

You ought to continuously attempt to stay away from any hereditarily changed food sources. Eating something that has been changed in a research center to be impervious to being broken up naturally will give your body's stomach related compounds trouble attempting to separate it as it has been altered to endure precisely that. Eat with your head and attempt to contemplate what you are placing into your body.

One of the most predominant suppositions about veganism is that you want creature items to source significant supplements, nutrients and minerals to carry on with a sound and healthy lifestyle. Investigate the beneath data for a sign of how a plant-based diet can adequately give you all that your body needs, without creature produce.

PROTEIN: Nuts, seeds, cereals, grains, beans, and soy (tofu or other soy based products) (tofu or other soy based products) CALCIUM: Dark mixed greens, nuts and seeds, new and dried foods grown from the ground wheat bread IRON: Leafy greens, wholemeal bread, grains, tofu/tempeh, lentils, and legumes POTASSIUM: White beans, potatoes (counting the skin), apricots, yogurt, bananas MAGNESIUM: Leafy greens, pumpkin seeds, earthy colored rice, dull chocolate VITAMIN C: Citrus, yellow chime peppers, kiwis, broccoli, strawberries, tomatoes VITAMIN A: Sweet potato, carrots, lettuce, paprika, mangoes, kale, dried apricots

Adopting a veggie lover diet doesn 't really mean you're naturally better. Regardless of whether you're veggie lover you could in fact live on sugar, Oreos, and french fries - so it's each of the an\s

issue of how you do it.

This book will motivate you to cook energizing, heavenly and flavorsome dishes while as yet following a sound way of life and giving your body sustenance. For instance, Chickpeas are great at keeping insulin levels stable, and that implies you will not get that lethargic inclination subsequent to eating. The Kung Pao Chickpea formula in this book is an ideal lunch or supper feast to keep you feeling full without that glucose plunge that you frequently get after a major dinner. The Vegetable Lo Mein is loaded with salad greens, assisting you with getting your suggested every day remittance of iron, potassium, and calcium.

For those with a sweet tooth, this formula book has a few truly scrumptious sweet treats, for example, Coconut Sticky Rice with Mango, Crispy Banana Fritters with Sesame Seeds or Ginger-mixed Japanese Rice Pudding.

Go straight to the recipe section.

NOURISH YOURSELF

Asian food best consolidates supplements from vegetables, heartbeats, and vegetables with the restorative characteristics of spices and flavors to make dinners that streamline the elements for solid eating.

Let's investigate a couple of normal Asian flavors and their wellbeing benefits:

CHILIES

Naturally high in L-ascorbic acid and a decent wellspring of Vitamin An and E. They go about as a blood purifier and are incredible for supporting absorption as well as assisting with mitigating headaches and throbbing muscles and joints.

TURMERIC

A strong cell reinforcement which additionally helps avert dementia and lessen the gamble of disease. It additionally creates a magnificently warm brilliant shading when added to curries.

GINGER

Aids great processing and dispenses with that swelled inclination after suppers. New ginger root is best as it tends to be ground and seared with your onions and adds a delectable lemony fragrance and flavor to curries.

CINNAMON

Excellent at directing glucose levels as well as lessening coronary illness and bringing down cholesterol. (Ensure you are utilizing Ceylon Cinnamon where possible)

CARDAMOM, CORIANDER, AND CUMIN

All assist with oxygenating your blood and add a gigantic flavorsome punch to Asian dishes.

GARLIC

A characteristic anti-toxin as well as adding a profound degree of flavor to food.

COCONUT MILK

Widely utilized as a base for curries, coconut milk is an extraordinary wellspring of magnesium and can assist with helping the insusceptible framework and advance weight reduction.

Individuals who are sensitive to tree nuts ought to constantly inquire as to whether a curry has coconut milk in it, as it can cause an unfavorably susceptible reaction.

SOY SAUCE

This is a staple in Japanese food and draws out a pungent, nutty and gritty flavor. You can get light soy that is utilized with sushi and dull soy that is utilized for cooking. The dull soy has a magnificent pungent caramel flavor that upgrades most foods.

MINT

Great at supporting assimilation as well as assisting with mitigating manifestations of IBS. The spice is a great method for cooling your mouth while eating a hot curry and furthermore makes a heavenly base for a plunging sauce with crude veggies.

CORIANDER

Dried cilantro flavor or cilantro leaves are utilized in curries as it has a sublime gritty taste. It is an incredible wellspring of dietary fiber as well as magnesium and L-ascorbic acid. The leaves of the new plant are known as Dhania and add a new and fresh flavor to curry. They can be placed on top as a topping and furthermore eaten with the curry.

LEMON GRASS

Commonly used to treat stomach throbs and hypertension, lemon grass is extraordinary at killing microorganisms so can be utilized to treat the normal virus. It smells summery and adds a newness to all Asian food, particularly curries.

ASIAN FUSION From eye-getting Sushi Rolls to warm and consoling Miso soup, you make certain to observe something to entice your taste buds in this cookbook. The plans in this book are not difficult to get ready utilizing ordinary fixings that you will find at your nearby supermarket.

Asian food is described by its place of beginning. The way of life of an Asian district decides the food varieties eaten around there. For instance, Japan is notable for aged soy items and rice and the Japanese gastronomy is the place where sushi starts from. A typical misnomer is that veggie lovers can't eat sushi. Assuming you take out the fish and utilize a vegetarian mayonnaise substitute you have a delectable, new and brilliantly quality dinner. You could involve the formula in this book to make your own sushi - that way you know precisely what goes into it. It will give you extraordinary regard for the Sushi ace at your neighborhood sushi restaurant!

The point of this formula book is to make eating better a lot more straightforward with the goal that it tends to be consolidated into your every day diet, and the vast majority of these plans take no longer than 30 minutes to get ready. The fixings utilized in this cookbook are direct, essential fixings. We've all been unmistakable extraordinary thing afterward stays in your cabinet until it surpasses the expiry date and you need to toss it in the container. By ensuring that every one of the fixings are not difficult to track down, you will actually want to source them rapidly and use them more regularly. You can likewise adjust the plans as you become more daring and energized at how incredible your eating change is making you feel.

baffled by plans that require a that requires days to source and Eating out in eateries can be a difficult encounter for a vegetarian. That is one of the incredible advantages of preparing Asian food at home. For the Eastern sense of taste comprehends that meat is only one element of a wide decision of many. There are such countless various preferences and flavors on proposition, and this book joins the most famous and exemplary dishes, making it the main veggie lover cookbook series you will need.

Go straight to the recipe section.

Chapter Three

EQUIPMENT WOK

The wok is by a long shot the main utensil while cooking Asian food. It is produced using weighty iron or steel and incredible when you really want to prepare a fast supper. This inward molded dish is exceptionally adaptable and ideal for sautéing, stewing or profound frying.

You can track down a decent quality wok at most stores, and consistently get one with a pleasant strong base so the hotness is uniformly dispersed. Watch the food preparing in a wok intently as it cooks quicker than traditional methods.

STEAMER

This is utilized for steaming rice, vegetables, buns, dumplings and to make faint total. It is an extremely helpful yet modest piece of gear and makes certain to be utilized habitually while preparing Asian food. A bamboo liner is the most customary kind of liner and has the extra advantage of steaming more than one layer of food simultaneously.

SUSHI MAT

The most straightforward, simple and secure strategy for making sushi is with a bamboo sushi mat. For a novice, creating sushi can be exceptionally baffling and also a muddled issue. On the off chance that you appreciate sushi and are probably going to make it a couple of times for yourself, your family or your companions it merits putting resources into a sushi mat.

BAMBOO SKEWERS

Great for barbecuing vegetables and tofu. Most usually utilized when vegetables or tofu have been marinated or enhanced, barbecued and afterward presented with satay sauce or sweet bean stew plunging sauce. Make certain to absorb the sticks water for around 10 minutes prior to piercing the tofu or veggies to keep them from burning.

Go straight to the recipe section.

PANTRY STAPLES

To make your life easier and to ensure your kitchen is equipt with staple items most commonly used in Asian cooking it is advisable that you have a well-stocked pantry to avoid a last minute trip to the supermarket after a long day at work.

The rundown beneath is an assortment of basic and direct fixings that you should keep in your pantries, prepared to prepare a flavorful colorful Asian dish at any time.

The 'F' image implies this can be frozen, decreasing how much waste and by keeping a very much loaded cooler you can guarantee you have these fixings to hand consistently. For best outcomes, you might have to check the most appropriate technique for freezing for the accompanying items.

LOVE VEGAN We love Asian food due to the fragile blend of fragrant flavors that make your taste buds sing.

This cookbook is centered around essential, regular and healthy fixings, and when cooked in the correct way and impeccably enhanced you can make wonderful, fascinating and mouth-watering veggie lover dishes, no matter what your cooking ability.

Whether you are a drawn out adherent of the vegetarian way of life, an amateur needing a simple method for getting everything rolling or a meateater hoping to join without meat Mondays into your week, this book will give you a few scrumptiously credible plans for any occasion.

So prepare for some colorful and simple to prepare vegetarian dinners that will open up a totally different world for you.

MAINS PERFECT PAD THAI Pad Thai begins from Thailand and is normally filled in as road food. This unquestionably basic and simple dish is overflowing with true flavors.

INGREDIENTS DIRECTIONS

In a medium estimated bowl drench the rice noodle for 30 minutes then, at that point, channel and set aside.

While the noodles are dousing make the nut sauce by consolidating all sauce fixings in a little pan and gradually heat to the point of boiling. Decrease to stew and cook for 2-3 minutes until the sauce thickens. Eliminate from the hotness and set aside.

Heat a huge skillet or wok over medium-high hotness and sautéed food ginger and garlic for 2-3 minutes. Diminish hotness to medium-low and add the noodles, sautéing for 2 minutes until they have softened.

Add the soy sauce, sugar, vinegar and paprika, mixing constantly.

Stir in the tofu and blend well to join all fixings, cooking for around 2-3 minutes. Add hoisin sauce, scallions, ground peanuts and bean sprouts, and ceaselessly mix to keep fixings from adhering to the lower part of the skillet. Pan sear for a further 3 minutes. Add a hint of water on the off chance that the dish has all the earmarks of being too dry.

Remove from the hotness and enhancement with scallions, bean sprouts, and a lime wedge and pour nut sauce over the top.

TAKE OUT STYLE CHOW MEIN

The great mix of delicate noodles and crunchy vegetables make this well known dish a genuine group pleaser. With just 5 minutes planning time, this feast can be on the supper table in a short time, making it an optimal dish for occupied weeknights.

DIRECTIONS

Bring a medium estimated pan loaded up with water to the bubble and cook noodles as indicated by parcel bearings, normally something like 5-6 minutes. Once cooked, channel and dispose of water.

While the noodles are cooking heat a huge wok with oil over medium hotness, and when hot add the onions, garlic, and stew. Saute for 2-3 minutes, add mushrooms, peas and bean grows then sautéed food for 4-5 minutes. Mix often to keep the vegetables from adhering to the bottom.

Add the noodles to the sautéed food, then, at that point, include soy sauce, rice vinegar, and brown sugar, blending great to consolidate. Cook for another 2-3 minutes and serve promptly while hot. Garnish with scallions.

SINGAPORE FRIED NOODLES

This solid Asian pan fried food is low in calories and stuffed brimming with flavor. It is suggested you cleave and set up each of the fixings in advance as you should work quick when mix frying.

DIRECTIONS

Soak noodles in a bowl of warm water for 15-20 minutes or plan as indicated by bundle headings. Channel well once cooked.

While noodles are drenching heat a huge wok or skillet with oil over medium-high hotness, then, at that point, add garlic and ginger. Saute for brief then, at that point, add curry powder and remaining vegetables, blending habitually.

Pan sear for 5 minutes or until the vegetables start to relax then add soy sauce, stew chips, and noodles. Cook briefly then add the coconut milk, guaranteeing all fixings are well combined. Remove from the hotness and serve immediately.

SWEET & SOUR VEGETABLE STIR-FRY

This formula consolidates tart and sweet flavors for a true hand crafted sauce that could match any take-out. It's stuffed brimming with vegetables and is a speedy and helpful dish to prepare for the entire family.

DIRECTIONS

Heat oil in a wok or container over medium-high hotness. When hot add onions and saute for 2-3 minutes, then, at that point, add garlic and fry for a further minute.

Add bok choy, cauliflower, carrot, tomato and peas and pan fried food for 1-2 minutes, moving the vegetables around continually to uniformly cook and keep them from adhering to the lower part of the pan.

Add pureed tomatoes, soy sauce and earthy colored sugar, and pan fried food briefly to permit the flavors to escalate. Pour in 1 cup of vegetable stock and heat to the point of boiling then, at that point, diminish to a simmer.

Add cornstarch to a little bowl and speed with 1 tbsp water to break up the starch and structure a thick paste.

Pour into the wok and cook for 5-7 minutes until the sauce thickens. Serve quickly while hot over newly cooked rice or noodles.

VEGETABLE LO MEIN

This straightforward yet flexible dish is brimming with vegetables and is solid and simple to make. Make certain to deplete your noodles a long time prior to adding them as wet noodles will make your pan fried food soggy.

INGREDIENTS

DIRECTIONS

In a little bowl whisk together the sauce fixings until all around consolidated and set aside. Bring a pot of water to a bubble and cook noodles as indicated by bundle directions.

While noodles are cooking heat an enormous wok or skillet over mediumhigh hotness and pan fried food the onions, ginger, and garlic for 30 seconds, then, at that point, add the

peppers and cook for a further 3-4 minutes until delicate. Add the noodles, Chinese greens, and scallions.

Pour in sauce and hotness for 1-2 minutes, blending admirably to guarantee all fixings are coated.

Add new spices then, at that point, eliminate from the hotness and serve immediately.

KAENG PHANAENG NEUA (PANANG CURRY)

This famous curry starts from Malaysia yet can be found in numerous locales around South East Asia. The sauce is rich and smooth, with a wonderful sweet-smelling flavor and a smidgen of chili.

INGREDIENTS

DIRECTIONS

To begin, eliminate tofu from bundling and press between two towels to eliminate abundance water. You can utilize something weighted, like an enormous pan or slashing board and put this on top of the tofu to press out however much dampness as could reasonably be expected for at least 10 minutes. This interaction will permit the tofu to ingest substantially more flavor.

Following 10 minutes cleave tofu into little cubes.

In an enormous wok or container heat oil over medium-high hotness. Add onions and saute for

2-3 minutes until delicate. Add ginger and garlic and cook for 1-2 minutes. Mix in curry glue and hotness for 1 moment to permit it to soften.

Pour in coconut milk, soy sauce, earthy colored sugar and lime squeeze and blend well to combine.

Add the broccoli, pepper, mushroom, tofu, and new spices and cook on a low stew for 10-15 minutes until the veggies and tofu and cooked all through and the sauce has thickened.

While the curry is cooking make the rice as indicated by the bundle bearings. Serve hot over rice and enhancement with cashew nuts and new herbs.

CREAMY THAI MASSAMAN CURRY

Massaman curry is implanted with extraordinary Thai flavors and consolidates a flawlessly rich and smooth sauce with sweet and nutty flavors. Albeit this curry utilizes numerous fixings there are not very many stages, making it a fast and simple feast to prepare.

INGREDIENTS DIRECTIONS

In a large saucepan heat oil over medium-high heat then saute onions for 2-3 minutes until soft. Add ginger and garlic and fry for 1 moment. Mix in carrot, cauliflower and beans and blend to consolidate. To some degree cover the dish and cook for 4 minutes until the vegetables have mellowed a little.

Add red pepper, curry glue and every one of the flavors. Fry for 2 minutes to relax the glue and meal the spices.

Mix in peanut butter, earthy colored sugar, soy sauce, coconut milk, and vegetable stock and consolidate well. Cover skillet and cook for 10 minutes, then, at that point, reveal and cook for a further 3-4 minutes or until the sauce thickens.

Season and add cleaved cilantro and lime juice. Serve quickly over newly cooked rice.

AUTHENTIC THAI GREEN CURRY

This famous dish is known for its sweet, fragrant and intriguing flavors. There's nothing more credible than making your own Thai Green Curry Paste and it will have a gigantic effect on the kind of the curry. You can twofold the glue formula and freeze it for up to a month.

INGREDIENTS

DIRECTIONS

In a blender add all curry glue fixings, with the exception of coconut milk, and heartbeat well until smooth. Add 1 tablespoon during a period of coconut milk to help the fixings join and structure a smooth yet thick paste.

In a huge wok or dish heat oil over medium-high hotness. When hot add glue and pan fried food for 1-2 minutes until fragrant.

Pour in stock, coconut milk and kaffir lime leaves and bring to a boil, then reduce to a low simmer. Add yams and tofu and stew for 6-8 minutes until the yam is delicate when punctured with a fork. This will rely upon how huge or little the potato 3D shapes are.

Add the zucchini and red pepper and cook for 5 minutes until the vegetables are delicate yet not soft. Blend in soy sauce and sugar.

Remove from the hotness, embellish with new basil and serve over newly cooked rice.

SPICY THAI PIZZA WITH PEANUT SATAY SAUCE

A fizzle resistant formula that demonstrates how to simple it is to make both the pizza batter and sauce totally without any preparation. The basic custom made satay beating truly makes this pizza exceptional and give it a sweet and nutty Thai flavor. The formula is for 2 hulls so you can freeze one for another day.

INGREDIENTS

FOR THE TOPPINGS

1 tbsp sesame oil

1 cup red onion, daintily cut 1 tbsp garlic, minced 1 tbsp ginger, minced

1 little red bean stew, deseeded and minced 7oz/200g mushrooms, sliced

½ a red pepper, meagerly sliced

8oz/230g firm tofu, cut into little cubes ½ cup peanuts Handful cleaved cilantro, chopped

DIRECTIONS

In a little bowl add water and sprinkle over yeast. Pass on to represent 5 minutes until froth begins to show up on the surface.

After 5 minutes add sugar, oil and salt, and delicately blend to join, then, at that point, move to the bowl of your stand mixer.

Using the batter snare gradually blend fixings while adding flour, ½ a cup at a time, until a thick mixture structures, around 4-5 minutes. Scrape down the edges and pull all the mixture in together. Sprinkle somewhat olive into the bowl and coat all sides of the dough. Cover with a kitchen towel and leave in a warm region for an hour.

After an hour the batter ought to have multiplied in size. Slice down the middle utilizing a blade and put the two pieces on a gently floured surface. Punch the mixture to deliver air and delicately manipulate briefly. Fold one of the pieces into a 12-inch round pizza mixture and gently brush with olive oil. Set aside.

You can freeze the other piece for later use by setting in a water/air proof zip lock bag.

TO MAKE THE SAUCE:

Place all fixings with the exception of cilantro in a little pan and cook over low

heat, mixing sporadically. Cook for 20 minutes or until the sauce has thickened and decreased. Eliminate from hotness and add hacked cilantro.

Preheat the stove to 220. Oil a baking plate with sesame oil.

While the sauce is cooking broil the tofu in the stove for 7-10 minutes until brown, turning the 3D squares following 5 minutes to guarantee they cook equally. Eliminate, however leave the broiler on at 220°c.

In a huge griddle or wok heat sesame oil over medium hotness. Pan sear onions, garlic, ginger and bean stew for 3 minutes, blending much of the time. Add mushrooms and red pepper and cook for a further 3-4 minutes until all vegetables have mellowed yet are not mushy.

Reduce hotness to low then, at that point, add half of the coconut sauce combination and mix to join. Heat the vegetables and sauce for 2-3 minutes.

Using an opened spoon spread combination over pizza mixture, making a point to cover the whole surface yet not adding an excess of sauce as your pizza will become soggy.

Top with peanuts and cilantro and prepare for 12-15 minutes. You can freeze any excess sauce.

GENERAL TSO'S CAULIFLOWER

This delicious dish joins sweet and fiery flavors with a tacky sauce that works out positively for rice. This veggie lover rendition replaces chicken with cauliflower and is loaded with vegetables, making this supper low calorie and healthy.

INGREDIENTS

DIRECTIONS

To start you want to marinate the cauliflower. In a large bowl whisk together soy sauce and sesame oil, then slowly add corn flour until a thick batter is formed. Add the cauliflower and blend until every floret is equitably covered. Leave to marinate for 15-20 minutes.

In an enormous skillet or wok heat 2 tbsp of nut or vegetable oil over medium-high heat.

Once the container is hot add the cauliflower blend in clumps and cook until delicately carmelized on all sides. You would rather not stuff the container so just fry a couple at a time. Shower more oil on the skillet assuming it gives off an impression of being staying. When firm exchange to a plate fixed with paper towels and set aside.

Using a similar skillet or wok saute ginger and garlic for 1 moment until fragrant, adding 1 tsp of oil if needed.

Add stock, soy sauce, corn flour, bean stew sauce, earthy colored sugar, and rice wine vinegar and mix until completely consolidated. Slowly bring mixture to a boil then reduce to a simmer. Mix regularly while the sauce thickens.

Once the sauce has thickened and become lustrous add the cauliflower and blend until every floret is covered with sauce.

Remove from heat, embellish with scallions and serve over white rice.

KUNG PAO CHICKPEAS

A Szechuan dish that is gently flavored with sweet, acrid and appetizing components. The fixings consolidate together to make a powerful and delightful feast that is straightforward and advantageous to make.

INGREDIENTS

DIRECTIONS

In an enormous bowl whisk together soy sauce, vinegar, lime, maple syrup, coconut oil and cornstarch until smooth. Add chickpeas and throw to consolidate. Cover the bowl and marinate in the refrigerator for at least 30 minutes. The more you can marinate the chickpeas for, the more flavor they will retain.

Heat coconut oil in a huge skillet or wok over medium-high hotness. Add the ginger and garlic and saute for 1-2 minutes. Mix in the chickpeas alongside the marinating sauce, kung pao sauce and stew drops. Cook for around 8 minutes, mixing frequently.

Once cooked eliminate from heat, move to a serving bowl and topping with cilantro, scallions and peanuts. Serve warm over newly cooked white rice.

Chapter Four

STICKY CHILI GARLIC TOFU

This basic dish is overflowing with bona fide Asian flavors. Squeezing the tofu in advance empowers it to assimilate considerably more flavor, and sautéing it gives it a brilliant fresh coating.

INGREDIENTS

VEGETABLE LO MEIN

This straightforward yet flexible dish is brimming with vegetables and is solid and simple to make. Make certain to deplete your noodles a long time prior to adding them as wet noodles will make your pan fried food soggy.

INGREDIENTS

DIRECTIONS

In a little bowl whisk together the sauce fixings until all around consolidated and set aside. Bring a pot of water to a bubble and cook noodles as indicated by bundle directions.

While noodles are cooking heat an enormous wok or skillet over mediumhigh hotness and pan fried food the onions, ginger, and garlic for 30 seconds, then, at that point, add the peppers and cook for a further 3-4 minutes until delicate. Add the noodles, Chinese greens, and scallions.

Pour in sauce and hotness for 1-2 minutes, blending admirably to guarantee all fixings are coated.

Add new spices then, at that point, eliminate from the hotness and serve immediately.

KAENG PHANAENG NEUA (PANANG CURRY)

This famous curry starts from Malaysia yet can be found in numerous locales around South East Asia. The sauce is rich and smooth, with a wonderful sweet-smelling flavor and a smidgen of chili.

INGREDIENTS

DIRECTIONS

To begin, eliminate tofu from bundling and press between two towels to eliminate abundance water. You can utilize something weighted, like an enormous pan or slashing board and put this on top of the tofu to press out however much dampness as could reasonably be expected for at least 10 minutes. This interaction will permit the tofu to ingest substantially more flavor.

Following 10 minutes cleave tofu into little cubes.

In an enormous wok or container heat oil over medium-high hotness. Add onions and saute for 2-3 minutes until delicate. Add ginger and garlic and cook for 1-2 minutes. Mix in curry glue and hotness for 1 moment to permit it to soften.

Pour in coconut milk, soy sauce, earthy colored sugar and lime squeeze and blend well to combine.

Add the broccoli, pepper, mushroom, tofu, and new spices and cook on a low stew for 10-15 minutes until the veggies and tofu and cooked all through and the sauce has thickened.

While the curry is cooking make the rice as indicated by the bundle bearings. Serve hot over rice and enhancement with cashew nuts and new herbs.

CREAMY THAI MASSAMAN CURRY

Massaman curry is implanted with extraordinary Thai flavors and consolidates a flawlessly rich and smooth sauce with sweet and nutty flavors. Albeit this curry utilizes numerous fixings there are not very many stages, making it a fast and simple feast to prepare.

INGREDIENTS DIRECTIONS

In a large saucepan heat oil over medium-high heat then saute onions for 2-3 minutes until soft. Add ginger and garlic and fry for 1 moment. Mix in carrot, cauliflower and beans and blend to consolidate. To some degree cover the dish and cook for 4 minutes until the vegetables have mellowed a little.

Add red pepper, curry glue and every one of the flavors. Fry for 2 minutes to relax the glue and meal the spices.

Mix in peanut butter, earthy colored sugar, soy sauce, coconut milk, and vegetable stock and consolidate well. Cover skillet and cook for 10 minutes, then, at that point, reveal and cook for a further 3-4 minutes or until the sauce thickens.

Season and add cleaved cilantro and lime juice. Serve quickly over newly cooked rice.

AUTHENTIC THAI GREEN CURRY

This famous dish is known for its sweet, fragrant and intriguing flavors. There's nothing more credible than making your own Thai Green Curry Paste and it will have a gigantic effect on the kind of the curry. You can twofold the glue formula and freeze it for up to a month.

INGREDIENTS

DIRECTIONS

In a blender add all curry glue fixings, with the exception of coconut milk, and heartbeat well until smooth. Add 1 tablespoon during a period of coconut milk to help the fixings join and structure a smooth yet thick paste.

In a huge wok or dish heat oil over medium-high hotness. When hot add glue and pan fried food for 1-2 minutes until fragrant.

Pour in stock, coconut milk and kaffir lime leaves and bring to a boil, then reduce to a low simmer. Add yams and tofu and stew for 6-8 minutes until the yam is delicate when punctured with a fork. This will rely upon how huge or little the potato 3D shapes are.

Add the zucchini and red pepper and cook for 5 minutes until the vegetables are delicate yet not soft. Blend in soy sauce and sugar.

Remove from the hotness, embellish with new basil and serve over newly cooked rice.

SPICY THAI PIZZA WITH PEANUT SATAY SAUCE

A fizzle resistant formula that demonstrates how to simple it is to make both the pizza batter and sauce totally without any preparation. The basic custom made satay beating truly makes this pizza exceptional and give it a sweet and nutty Thai flavor. The formula is for 2 hulls so you can freeze one for another day.

INGREDIENTS

FOR THE TOPPINGS

1 tbsp sesame oil

1 cup red onion, daintily cut 1 tbsp garlic, minced 1 tbsp ginger, minced 1 little red bean stew, deseeded and minced 7oz/200g mushrooms, sliced ½ a red pepper, meagerly sliced 8oz/230g firm tofu, cut into little cubes ½ cup peanuts Handful cleaved cilantro, chopped

DIRECTIONS

In a little bowl add water and sprinkle over yeast. Pass on to represent 5 minutes until froth begins to show up on the surface.

After 5 minutes add sugar, oil and salt, and delicately blend to join, then, at that point, move to the bowl of your stand mixer.

Using the batter snare gradually blend fixings while adding flour, ½ a cup at a time, until a thick mixture structures, around 4-5 minutes. Scrape down the edges and pull all the mixture in together. Sprinkle somewhat olive into the bowl and coat all sides of the dough. Cover with a kitchen towel and leave in a warm region for an hour.

After an hour the batter ought to have multiplied in size. Slice down the middle utilizing a blade and put the two pieces on a gently floured surface. Punch the mixture to deliver air and delicately manipulate briefly. Fold one of the pieces into a

12-inch round pizza mixture and gently brush with olive oil. Set aside. You can freeze the other piece for later use by setting in a water/air proof zip lock bag.

TO MAKE THE SAUCE:

Place all fixings with the exception of cilantro in a little pan and cook over low heat, mixing sporadically. Cook for 20 minutes or until the sauce has thickened and decreased. Eliminate from hotness and add hacked cilantro.

Preheat the stove to 220. Oil a baking plate with sesame oil.

While the sauce is cooking broil the tofu in the stove for 7-10 minutes until brown, turning the 3D squares following 5 minutes to guarantee they cook equally. Eliminate, however leave the broiler on at 220°c.

In a huge griddle or wok heat sesame oil over medium hotness. Pan sear onions, garlic, ginger and bean stew for 3 minutes, blending much of the time. Add mushrooms and red pepper and cook for a further 3-4 minutes until all vegetables have mellowed yet are not mushy.

Reduce hotness to low then, at that point, add half of the coconut sauce combination and mix to join. Heat the vegetables and sauce for 2-3 minutes.

Using an opened spoon spread combination over pizza mixture, making a point to cover the whole surface yet not adding an excess of sauce as your pizza will become soggy.

Top with peanuts and cilantro and prepare for 12-15 minutes. You can freeze any excess sauce.

GENERAL TSO'S CAULIFLOWER

This delicious dish joins sweet and fiery flavors with a tacky sauce that works out positively for rice. This veggie lover rendition replaces chicken with cauliflower and is loaded with vegetables, making this supper low calorie and healthy.

INGREDIENTS

DIRECTIONS

To start you want to marinate the cauliflower. In a large bowl whisk together soy sauce and sesame oil, then slowly add corn flour until a thick batter is formed. Add the cauliflower and blend until every floret is equitably covered. Leave to marinate for 15-20 minutes.

In an enormous skillet or wok heat 2 tbsp of nut or vegetable oil over medium-high heat.

Once the container is hot add the cauliflower blend in clumps and cook until delicately carmelized on all sides. You would rather not stuff the container so just fry a couple at a time. Shower more oil on the skillet assuming it gives off an impression of being staying. When firm exchange to a plate fixed with paper towels and set aside.

Using a similar skillet or wok saute ginger and garlic for 1 moment until fragrant, adding 1 tsp of oil if needed.

Add stock, soy sauce, corn flour, bean stew sauce, earthy colored sugar, and rice wine vinegar and mix until completely consolidated. Slowly bring mixture to a boil then reduce to a simmer. Mix regularly while the sauce thickens.

Once the sauce has thickened and become lustrous add the cauliflower and blend until every floret is covered with sauce.

Remove from heat, embellish with scallions and serve over white rice.

KUNG PAO CHICKPEAS

A Szechuan dish that is gently flavored with sweet, acrid and appetizing components. The fixings consolidate together to make a powerful and delightful feast that is straightforward and advantageous to make.

DIRECTIONS

To begin, eliminate tofu from bundling and press between two towels to eliminate abundance water. You can use something weighted, such as a large saucepan or a heavy chopping board and place this on top of the tofu to squeeze out as much moisture as possible for a minimum of 10 minutes. This cycle will permit the tofu to ingest significantly more flavor. Following 10 minutes cleave tofu into little cubes.

In a skillet or wok add soy sauce, hoisin sauce, and garlic and mix until all around consolidated. Add tofu and blend until each piece is entirely covered. Eliminate from the hotness, and move to the refrigerator in a covered bowl for at least 20 minutes.

Meanwhile, cook the rice according to packet directions then drain and cover with a towel once cooked. In a skillet or wok heat 2 tablespoons of oil over medium hotness. Add marinated tofu in a solitary layer alongside the sauce and fry without mixing for 5 minutes. Flip every tofu 3D square and cook on the opposite side for 5 minutes. Add the scallions throughout the previous 2 minutes of cooking.

Serve over warm rice and embellishment with sesame seeds if using.

SWEET POTATO TERIYAKI WITH FLUFFY CAULIFLOWER RICE

Cauliflower rice, in place of white rice, cuts the calories in half and provides for a very flavorful meal since it is so good at absorbing flavor. This Japanese-inspired recipe combines a sweet, tangy sauce with plenty of veggies, making it a simple and healthy meal for the whole family.

INGREDIENTS

DIRECTIONS

Preheat the oven to 200 degrees Fahrenheit. Using a little amount of oil, coat a baking dish and set aside. Combine the diced yam and teriyaki sauce in a large mixing basin.

soy sauce with sriracha sauce Prepare under the broiler for 30-35 minutes, mixing occasionally, until evenly covered. Remove the potatoes from the broiler when they are tender but not mushy when poked with a fork.

Make the cauliflower rice while the potatoes are cooking. Fill a food processor halfway with cauliflower and pulse in short bursts until the cauliflower resembles rice grains. It's important not to overwork this since a puree isn't required. If you don't have a food processor, use a hand handled grater to shred the cauliflower.

Combine cauliflower rice, ginger, and garlic in a microwave-safe bowl. Cover and microwave for 4-5 minutes, or until the rice is tender and the cauliflower is fully cooked. Remove from the equation.

When the yams are done, transfer them to a large serving dish and mix with the scallions, corn, edamame, sesame seeds, and avocado. Toss to combine and serve over cauliflower rice while still warm.

FRESH SUMMER ROLLS FROM VIETNAM

These light, fresh, and divine rolls are a mainstay in Vietnam, and a welcome contrast from the more common rotisserie varieties. The rolls are fantastic as an appetizer and surprisingly satisfying as a meal on their own. Bahn Trang is a rice paper coating that may be purchased in Asian stores.

INGREDIENTS

DIRECTIONS

In a medium-sized mixing basin, soak noodles in boiling water for 3-4 minutes before channeling and setting aside.

In a separate basin filled with warm water, moisten both sides of rice paper sheets one at a time. Remove from the water, brushing off any excess, and place in a single layer on a clean work surface or cleaving board.

EACH ROLL MUST BE ASSEMBLED IN THE FOLLOWING ORDER:

Place a lettuce leaf, rice noodles, a cilantro and mint branch, a little red cabbage, a spoonful of ground carrots, three cucumber sticks, and a sprinkling of sesame seeds on a plate. If you pack the rolls too tightly, they will be difficult to roll.

Pull the bottom edge of the covering up over the filling firmly. Fold the edges inside over it. Continue to push yourself up and over to a large plate with the crease side down. Re-create the dish using the remaining components.

Serve with a sweet stew or a nut plunging sauce as a side dish.

The rolls may be served right once or stored in the refrigerator with a little dampened rag draped over them to prevent drying. If you don't plan on serving them for at least an hour, cover the plate and soggy material with cling wrap and put them in the refrigerator.

SKEWERS OF TOFU WITH SATAY SAUCE

A simple recipe for fresh, delicate tofu encased in a sweet, velvety nut satay sauce that is flavorful to the max. The satay sauce is a fantastic pantry staple that can be poured over veggies, used in pan-fried dishes, or used as a noodle sauce.

INGREDIENTS

DIRECTIONS

To begin, remove the tofu from the packaging and press it between two towels to absorb excess moisture. Place something heavy on top of the tofu, such as a big saucepan or a hefty chopping board, to push out as much liquid as possible for at least 10 minutes. This process will allow the tofu to retain a lot more taste. After 10 minutes, cut the tofu into cubes.

In a medium bowl, combine soy sauce, sesame oil, water, vinegar, garlic, and ginger after the tofu has been pressed, then add tofu, gently tossing to ensure each cube is properly coated in the marinade. Allow to marinate for 10-15 minutes, or for as little time as possible.

While the tofu is marinating, create the satay sauce. Heat sesame oil in a heavy-bottomed pan over medium heat, then add garlic and ginger, mixing constantly for a few seconds. Mix together the peanut butter, sugar, and coconut milk until the peanut butter is completely dissolved. Cook for 5-10 minutes over low heat, until the sauce has thickened, adding the soy sauce, lime juice, and stew drops as needed. Remove from the heat and put aside.

Preheat the grill to high.

Thread the pre-splashed wooden sticks with your preferred tofu shapes and pepper (if you don't saturate them, they will burn under the grill).

Grill the sticks for 5-7 minutes, flipping them often to ensure that each side is roasted and the tofu does not burn.

Serve with a satay sauce that is still heated.

GINGER PEANUT DRIZZLE ON CRUNCHY CASHEW COCONUT RICE

This Thai-inspired rice salad is made appealing by crunchy cashew nuts, creamy coconut rice, and crispy veggies. It stays nicely in the fridge and is perfect for a light lunch, particularly when drizzled with peanut ginger.

DIRECTIONS FOR INGREDIENTS

In a medium saucepan, combine the coconut milk, garlic, and stock; cover and bring to a boil. When the liquid starts to boil, add the rice and reduce to a stew. Cover and cook for 17 minutes, without opening the lid. When the concocting time is over, remove from the heat and allow it rest for a further 10 minutes with the lid on.

You may prepare the nut sauce while the rice is cooking. Combine peanut butter and earthy colored sugar in a small saucepan over medium heat until smooth. Allowing the mixture to simmer or bubble is not a good idea. Blend in the ginger, rice vinegar, sesame oil, and red wine vinegar (if using). Thin with water until the desired consistency is achieved, then add lime juice. Remove from the equation.

Combine all of the cut vegetables and cashew nuts in a large serving dish. Rice should be cushioned with a fork before being added to the veggies and well blended. Serve warm with a nut sauce drizzled over top.

SUSHI ROLLS WITH QUINOA, AVOCADO, AND SPINACH

Sushi has a reputation for being difficult to prepare; however, this recipe is simple to follow and incorporates fresh and substantial ingredients for a tasty and full lunch.

INGREDIENTS

DIRECTIONS

Fill a kettle halfway with water and heat to a rolling boil. Reduce to a delicate stew, cover, and simmer for 15-17 minutes, or until all the water has been absorbed.

While the quinoa is cooking, combine rice vinegar, maple syrup (or sugar), and salt in a small bowl. Remove from the equation.

When the quinoa has finished cooking, fluff it with a fork and transfer it from the saucepan to a large platter. 1 tablespoon at a time, add the vinegar-soy mixture to the quinoa and stir until thoroughly incorporated.

Place a nori sheet on a sushi mat and evenly sprinkle 14 of the quinoa mix over the sheet, with the exception of the final two creeps, which should be hosed to adhere.

Top with a handful of spinach and slices of cucumber and avocado. Roll tightly, and as you near the finish, moisten the end strip with your fingertips, pressing down delicately to make it cling. Re-roll with the remaining fixes until you have a total of four rolls.

Cut each roll evenly into four sushi pieces with a razor-sharp knife.

Serve immediately with wasabi, or preserve in an airtight container in the refrigerated for up to 3 days.

SPICY SICHUAN EGGPLANT This meal combines the Sichuan region's spicy and fiery characteristics. The eggplants are pan-seared to create a delicate, velvety surface that contrasts well with the sweet and savory sauce.

INGREDIENTS

INSTRUCTIONS INSTRUCTIONS INSTRUCTIONS INSTRUCTION

After 4 minutes, add the eggplant and cook for another 4 minutes. Mix in the salt and the stew chunks every now and then. Cook for 6-8 minutes, or until the eggplant is tender but not overcooked. Place the mixture in a basin and put it aside. 1 tbsp coconut oil, heated in a similar dish, garlic and ginger, sauteed for 2-3 minutes.

Combine sesame seeds, pureed tomatoes, earthy colored sugar, stew sauce, molasses, soy sauce, rice vinegar, white vinegar, and water in a large mixing bowl. Consolidate well and cook for 10 minutes on low heat until the sauce thickens. Combine the eggplant and sliced cilantro in the sauce and mix to combine the flavors, fricasseeing for about 5 minutes.

Remove from the heat and serve over white rice, garnished with scallions.

LAKSA MALAYSIAN

Laksa is a spicy coconut noodle soup that's bursting at the seams with flavor. This delicious and genuine recipe makes a quick laksa pasta using fresh ingredients, eliminating the need for store-bought bottled laksa. Because the laksa paste can be frozen, you may prepare double and save half for next night's meal.

INGREDIENTS

DIRECTIONS

Heat the oil in a pan over medium heat, then add the cumin and cilantro seeds, stirring constantly. Fry for a few minutes, or until aromatic, then add the shallots. Cook for 3-4 minutes, or until they've softened, then add the garlic and ginger and mix quickly. Mix the shallot mixture with any residual laksa paste ingredients in a food processor or fast blender until you get a fine paste.

Heat 3-4 tbsp laksa glue in a large saucepan with sesame oil (begin with 3 and add the fourth later whenever you have tried the hotness). In a large mixing bowl, combine the vegetable stock, coconut milk, soy sauce, lime leaves, and earthy colored sugar. Bring to a boil slowly.

Reduce the heat to a simmer, then add the kid corn, zucchini, and carrots and cook for 10 minutes, or until tender.

While the veggies are resting, prepare the noodles according to the package directions, then add them to the broth.

Remove from the heat and stir in the bean sprouts and cilantro. Serve immediately while still hot, garnished with sesame seeds.

The laksa adhesive will keep for a long time in the refrigerator or for a long period in the cooler. The laksa soup will keep in an airtight container for three days, and you will find it to be even more wonderful as the flavors combine.

PHO IN VIETNAMESE

Pho is a fragrant noodle soup made with aromatic spices, fresh herbs, and veggies from Vietnam. It's light yet filling, and it's quite simple to prepare at home. This vegan version has more veggies, making it a filling and fulfilling dinner.

INGREDIENTS

DIRECTIONS

Pour sesame oil into a big saucepan. When the pan is heated, add the onions and cook for 3-4 minutes, or until they are soft. Cook for 1-2 minutes, until aromatic, adding ginger and garlic as needed.

Cook for a few minutes on medium-high with the shiitake mushrooms. Mix in the lemongrass, cinnamon, scallions, and fennel until all flavors are well distributed.

Add vegetable stock, water, soy sauce, rice wine vinegar, and salt after 2-3 minutes. Bring to a boil, then reduce to a simmer for 30 minutes. The longer you simmer the soup, the richer the flavors get.

Pho is traditionally pressed before serving, with fennel, onions, mushrooms, and other veggies removed, but you may leave the vegetables in for a heartier, more substantial soup.

With the noodles and toppings, garnish and serve.

MISO SOUP QUICK & EASY

This Miso Soup comes together quickly with just 6 ingredients. It's refreshing and light, and it makes a lovely snack or full meal. Make sure to use Miso glue that does not include bonito (fish taste), since this is a non-vegetarian fixation. If you can't get nori, skip it; nonetheless, it adds another layer of genuine taste.

INGREDIENTS

1 cup dull green leaf (green chard, bok choy, etc.) 12 cup firm tofu, sliced into tiny cubes 1 cup chopped scallions

white miso glue, 6-8 tbsp (aged soybean paste)

12 cup nori (dry seaweed) or 2 sheets nori (split into large squares) 8 oz.

DIRECTIONS

Carry water to a low simmer in a large pan, add nori, and cook for 6 to 8 minutes.

Place the miso glue in a small dish, add a few tablespoons of warm water, and whisk until smooth while the nori is stewing. Toss salad leaves, scallions, and tofu into the heated soup with the glue.

Allow to simmer for 10-15 minutes, covered, over a low heat. Warm it up and serve.

For up to 5 days, the soup may be stored in a sealed container in the refrigerator.

GYOZA is a Japanese word that means "good luck" (JAPANESE DUMPLINGS)

These delectable small dumplings are packed with luscious veggies and fried first, leaving one side crisp while the other is tenderly steamed. When preparing these again, you might prepare an additional part of the filling and freeze it to save time.

INGREDIENTS

THE FILLING INSTRUCTIONS:

In a large griddle, heat the oil and sauté the garlic and ginger until fragrant, about 1 minute. Combine the cabbage, mushrooms, carrots, and tofu in a large mixing bowl. Cook for another 4-5 minutes, or until the veggies and tofu have softened. Soy sauce, rice wine vinegar, and stock should all be added at this point. Allow it simmer for 5-6 minutes, stirring often, after blending to consolidate.

Add cornstarch, ½ tbsp at a time and mix well after every option. Remove from the hotness and permit to chill off for 10-15 minutes until sufficiently cool to touch.

FOR THE GYOZA:

Have every one of the things prepared as this will make the interaction a lot simpler. You will require the filling, the gyoza coverings and a little bowl of water to wet your fingers. Heat vegetable oil in a container with a top. Set up the coverings by spreading them out in a solitary layer on a spotless work surface while the oil is warming up.

Scoop around 1 tbsp of the combination into your hands and utilize your palms fold it into a ball. Place the chunk of combination in the focal point of a gyoza covering, wet at the tip of your finger and follow a line around the edges of a large portion of the covering. Presently overlay the covering in half over the filling and squeeze the enveloping together utilizing your pointer and thumb by request to seal it.

Place all the Gyoza dumplings in the hot oil simultaneously, with the crease side looking up, add a little water to conceal to 1/3 of the Gyoza. Cover the container and cook over medium-high hotness for 3-4 minutes. While the gyoza is steaming combine the sauce fixings as one involving a whisk and spot in a shallow bowl appropriate for dipping.

Once the water has diminished to half, reveal the container and cook until the rest of the water has vanished. The gyoza are done once the lower part of the dumplings have browned.

Transfer to a huge serving plate alongside plunging sauce.

Sorry to bother you, but you seem like the helpful type :-)

If you have 2 minutes spare, we'd be so appreciative if you would leave us a speedy audit, as surveys are significant and will permit us to continue to make incredible quality cookbooks!

SIDES NASU DENGAKU (MISO GLAZED EGGPLANT)

This exemplary Japanese side dish highlights delicate eggplants with a sweet and appetizing tacky miso coat and finished off with sesame seeds. It's extraordinary filled in as a side dish or even as a fundamental course with steamed rice.

INGREDIENTS

4 little eggplants

1 tsp salt

½ cup hatcho miso or 2 tbsp white + 2 tbsp red miso combined as one 4 tbsp mirin 1 tbsp rice vinegar

1 tbsp maple syrup or sugar 2 tsp sesame oil 4 tbsp sesame seeds

DIRECTIONS

Slice the eggplants into equal parts, lengthways, as equitably as could really be expected. Sprinkle salt onto within the eggplant and leave for 30 minutes for the salt to eliminate any harshness. Flush with cold water and wipe off, eliminating however much abundance water as could be expected with a kitchen towel.

Score the eggplant slantingly in the two bearings (a jumble design) to make little squares utilizing a sharp knife.

Preheat the barbecue. Brush the eggplant with a little sesame oil and put on a foil lined baking plate in your broiler, for 10 minutes, turning over once after 5 minutes.

Remove the eggplants, brush liberally with the miso coating and spot back in the stove for 3-4 minutes. Watch out for the eggplants as they are inclined to

burning.

Remove from the stove and sprinkle every half with ½ tablespoon of sesame seeds. Serve promptly while hot.

CHINESE SPECIAL FRIED RICE

The secret to this dish is to use leftover cold rice. It absorbs so much more of the flavor and gives the dish that authentic texture that you find in restaurants. If you do not have leftover rice, simply boil a batch, spread it over a large plate and leave it in the fridge for 30 minutes to cool down before cooking. The recipe also uses frozen vegetables, making this super quick and easy to whip up.

INGREDIENTS

Once the water has diminished to half, reveal the container and cook until the rest of the water has vanished. The gyoza are done once the lower part of the dumplings have browned.

Transfer to a huge serving plate alongside plunging sauce.

Sorry to bother you, but you seem like the helpful type :-)

If you have 2 minutes spare, we'd be so appreciative if you would leave us a speedy audit, as surveys are significant and will permit us to continue to make incredible quality cookbooks!

SIDES NASU DENGAKU (MISO GLAZED EGGPLANT) (MISO GLAZED EGGPLANT)

This exemplary Japanese side dish highlights delicate eggplants with a sweet and appetizing tacky miso coat and finished off with sesame seeds. It's extraordinary filled in as a side dish or even as a fundamental course with steamed rice.

INGREDIENTS

4 little eggplants

1 tsp salt

½ cup hatcho miso or 2 tbsp white + 2 tbsp red miso combined as one 4 tbsp mirin 1 tbsp rice vinegar

1 tbsp maple syrup or sugar 2 tsp sesame oil 4 tbsp sesame seeds

DIRECTIONS

Slice the eggplants into equal parts, lengthways, as equitably as could really be expected. Sprinkle salt onto within the eggplant and leave for 30 minutes for the salt to eliminate any harshness. Flush with cold water and wipe off, eliminating however much abundance water as could be expected with a kitchen towel.

Score the eggplant slantingly in the two bearings (a jumble design) to make little squares utilizing a sharp knife.

Preheat the barbecue. Brush the eggplant with a little sesame oil and put on a foil lined baking plate in your broiler, for 10 minutes, turning over once after 5 minutes.

Remove the eggplants, brush liberally with the miso coating and spot back in the stove for 3-4 minutes. Watch out for the eggplants as they are inclined to\sburning.

Remove from the stove and sprinkle every half with ½ tablespoon of sesame seeds. Serve promptly while hot.

CHINESE SPECIAL FRIED RICE

The secret to this dish is to use leftover cold rice. It absorbs so much more of the flavor and gives the dish that authentic texture that you find in restaurants. If you do not have leftover rice, simply boil a batch, spread it over a large plate and leave it in the fridge for 30 minutes to cool down before cooking. The recipe also uses frozen vegetables, making this super quick and easy to whip up.

INGREDIENTS

DIRECTIONS

Heat oil in an enormous wok over medium-high hotness. Add onions and saute for 2-3 minutes until delicate, then, at that point, add ginger and garlic and cook for a further minute.

Add frozen vegetables and cook until thawed out and warmed all through, around 3-4 minutes. Mix in mushrooms and saute while oftentimes stirring.

Add turmeric and blend well to join, then, at that point, toss in cool rice and mix continually to fuse all fixings and separate any bunches. Pour in soy sauce. Serve immediately.

JAPANESE TEMPURA

Tempura is a Japanese dish consisting of either seafood or vegetables which have been battered in a very light and crisp coating. Our appetising vegan version uses sparkling water to ensure the batter stays light and crisp.

INGREDIENTS

DIRECTIONS

Heat the oil in an enormous pot or wok until it arrives at 350°c. Make sure every one of the vegetables are prepared and the oil is hot before you make the batter.

Whisk together the flour, cornstarch and salt then add the carbonated water and whisk until just combined then add the ice cubes. The way to making incredible tempura is to not over whisk the hitter, it is fine in the event that irregularities remain. You ought to likewise work quick and utilize the hitter promptly to guarantee it remains cold.

Dip the vegetables into the batter, one at a time, then carefully drop them into the oil. Try not to sear such a large number of immediately as this will lessen the temperature of the oil bringing about your tempura not getting firm. Cook each piece for 1-2 minutes, going once to guarantee they are equally cooked.

Remove with an opened spoon and move to a paper towel lined plate. Serve promptly once all the tempura have cooked.

TOD MAN KHAO POD (THAI CORN FRITTERS) (THAI CORN FRITTERS)

These wastes are stove prepared rather than singed, making them a lot better yet as yet holding the fresh and crunchy external covering. There are not very many advances engaged with this formula and it just requires 10 minutes to prepare.

INGREDIENTS

DIRECTIONS

Place tofu in a food processor or blender and heartbeat until it has become smooth. Remove from the equation. Preheat the stove to 170°c. Oil a baking plate with a little oil or line with material paper.

In a huge bowl consolidate pounded tofu, corn, flour, cornstarch, baking powder, scallions, cilantro, lime zing, soy sauce, red curry glue, bean stew drops and water. Blend well until a thick hitter has framed and all fixings are completely blended together.

Use an enormous spoon or frozen yogurt scoop to shape player into a round shape and straighten a little with your hands or utilizing the rear of a spoon to frame a fritter.

Place on the baking plate and rehash with remaining batter.

Bake for 27-30 minutes until edges have seared. Flip squander over following 15 minutes of cooking.

Serve promptly while hot and crispy.

CRUNCHY ASIAN SALAD WITH SWEET SESAME VINAIGRETTE

This vibrant, colorful and delicious salad is an Asian twist on a classic recipe which replaces rice with quinoa. It's loaded with veggies and is bursting with flavor from the addition of the Asian Vinaigrette.

INGREDIENTS

DIRECTIONS

Bring 2 cups water to a moving bubble then, at that point, add quinoa. Diminish to a delicate stew and cook covered for 17-20 minutes or as indicated by bundle headings. When cooked eliminate from hotness and cushion up utilizing a fork.

In a huge serving bowl add all coleslaw fixings together and throw until well combined. To make the vinaigrette whisk all fixings together.

Sprinkle vinaigrette over salad and serve.

The plate of mixed greens will keep in an impermeable holder in the ice chest for 2 days.

CHILI GARLIC MUSHROOMS

This easy side dish combines exotic flavors with a spicy kick. Stir-frying enables the mushrooms to be cooked to perfection and makes this a quick and easy dish using ingredients you are likely to already have in your cupboard.

INGREDIENTS

DIRECTIONS

Heat oil in a griddle or wok over medium-high hotness. When hot add garlic and saute for 30 seconds. Add mushrooms, parsley, bean stew, lemon juice, sherry and soy sauce.

Stir-fry for 5-6 minutes until the mushrooms are cooked all through. Mix continually to keep the mushrooms from consuming. Assuming that the blend is adhering to the lower part of the container add a sprinkle of water.

Season with salt and pepper and serve quickly while hot.

SAUTÉED BROCCOLI WITH ASIAN GARLIC SAUCE

Fragrant garlic and firm broccoli make this dish a top pick for focus points and in cafés. You can undoubtedly reproduce this delicious conventional dish in your own kitchen and it won't take you more than 10 minutes.

INGREDIENTS

DIRECTIONS

In a little bowl whisk together garlic, ginger and soy sauce.

Heat oil in a wok or skillet over medium-high hotness and add broccoli. Pan sear for 3-4 minutes, blending continually to keep the florets from adhering to the lower part of the pan.

Reduce hotness to medium-low and pour in soy sauce and cornstarch combination, mixing admirably to cover the entirety of the broccoli. Continue to mix for around 3 minutes for the sauce to thicken. Taste and season with salt and pepper if required.

Remove from hotness and serve promptly while hot.

SOFT CHINESE BAO BUNS

A baozi (bao bun) is a cushioned steamed bun with a soy bean glue filling that is extremely famous in Asian cooking. The bun is fragile and light with a flavorful focus, that can be eaten as a tidbit or filled in as a side dish to go with a fundamental meal.

INGREDIENTS

DIRECTIONS

In a little bowl add warm water (assuming you have a cooking thermometer the water should be 35°c) and delicately mix in the yeast. Put away for 5 minutes. You should see little air pockets framing at the surface.

In a huge bowl add the flour then, at that point, gradually pour in the water-yeast mixture, blending with a wooden spoon.

On a clean, daintily floured surface manipulate the batter with your hands for 5-6 minutes. It very well might be somewhat tacky from the outset however keep on tidying the surface with a little flour at a time and it should begin meeting up. Place in a huge bowl, cover with a fabric and pass on to rest in a dry region for 1 hour or until the batter pairs in size. After an hour move to a gently floured surface again and punch the air out by driving your clench hand into the focal point of the mixture, pulling it back into a ball shape and rehashing a couple times.

Roll the batter out into a long log of around 1-inch in width and utilizing a blade cut the sign into little bits of around 1-inch long. Straighten these with your hands or by squeezing them with the rear of a cup to shape a dainty round 'coin'. These are called baozi and are to be utilized as coverings. Remember they should be adequately huge to load up with stuffing. Put away in a solitary layer on an enormous plate or your kitchen work surface while you set up the filling.

Heat oil in a wok or dish over medium-high hotness, and when hot add ginger, garlic and bean glue, mixing continually for 1 moment until fragrant.

Add tofu, salt, and soy sauce and blend well. Pan sear for a further 5-7 minutes until the tofu is cooked. Add scallions then, at that point, eliminate from the heat.

Prepare your steamer.

Place one loaded tablespoon of the filling into the focal point of the baozi and start to crease the edges clockwise, squeezing the covering as you come. Move your thumb and pointer around in a clockwise bearing, squeezing the covering together until the bun is sealed.

Lightly brush the bun with a few oil on the top and base and spot in the liner. Rehash with residual coverings and filling.

Steam buns for 15 minutes. Serve quickly while warm.

COCONUT & LIME RICE

Coriander, coconut, and lime transform plain rice into a delicately flavored and exotic side dish, perfect to accompany a curry or main meal.

DIRECTIONS FOR INGREDIENTS

In a large saucepan bring salt, pepper, coconut milk and water to a boil then add the rice. Stir to combine and release any grains that have stuck to the bottom of the saucepan then reduce heat to a low simmer and cook covered for 14-17 minutes.

Remove from the hotness and mix in lime zing, lime juice and cilantro. Utilize a fork to cushion the rice up.

Serve quickly while channeling hot.

COCONUT CRUSTED TOFU BITES WITH CREAMY THAI GREEN SAUCE

This tasty bite-sized finger food can be served as an appetizer or as a side dish. The sweet crusty coating is made with shredded coconut and cashew nuts, and the bites are then dipped into a beautifully creamy and exotically flavored sauce.

INGREDIENTS

DIRECTIONS

To begin, remove the tofu from the packaging and press it between two towels to absorb excess moisture. You can utilize something weighted, like an enormous pot or slashing board and put this on top of the tofu to press out however much dampness as could reasonably be expected for at least 10 minutes. This process will allow the tofu to retain a lot more taste. Following 10 minutes slash tofu into little scaled down cubes.

FOR THE DIPPING SAUCE:

While the tofu is being squeezed make the sauce. In a little pan consolidate coconut milk, green curry glue, pineapple juice, earthy colored sugar, and lime zing over medium-low hotness. When the fluid begins to stew eliminate 2 tbsp and\smove into a little bowl. Race in cornstarch or arrowroot powder until a smooth glue is shaped then empty once again into coconut milk coconut milk 7 minutes.

Remove from the hotness, move to a little serving bowl and permit to cool to room temperature. This sauce can be made as long as one day ahead, shrouded in saran wrap and left in the refrigerator overnight.

FOR THE COCONUT TOFU BITES:

Preheat the broiler to 190°c. Line a baking plate with material paper and shower with nonstick splash or oil with a little coconut oil.

In a medium bowl whisk mustard, coconut milk, lime, sugar, and salt until all around consolidated. Place cubed tofu in the combination and utilize a spatula to guarantee each piece is\s

covered. Pass on to absorb the flavor for at least 10 minutes.

In a shallow dish or enormous plate pour in the parched coconut and cashew nuts and blend well. Dunk every tofu piece into the coconutcashew blend and roll around to uniformly cover each side. Make a point to permit any overabundance coconut-mustard blend to trickle off prior to covering to keep the parched coconut from turning into a tacky mess.

Place every coconut crusted piece on the baking plate and rehash with outstanding tofu. Heat for 25-30 minutes, turning once following 15 minutes, until brilliant brown. Serve right away or permit to cool to room temperature.

DESSERTS COCONUT MATCHA TARTS

Finally, a pastry that is sound! The outside layer is produced using oats, coconut, and buckwheat flour, and the smooth and rich filling highlights crude cashew nuts, coconut cream, and very solid matcha. The expansion of matcha powder gives the filling a brilliantly lively green color.

INGREDIENTS

* FOR THE COCONUT CREAM: This should either be the assortment you can purchase in a hard square or you can take a container of full-fat coconut milk, place it in the cooler short-term and utilize the hard cream that will have framed at the top.

DIRECTIONS

FOR THE CRUST:

Preheat the stove to 350° F. Line the foundation of 4 ramekins (around 4.5 inches in\sdistance across) with material paper and oil the edges with around 1 teaspoon of coconut oil and set aside.

Place oats and coconut in a food processor or fast blender and heartbeat until it turns into a fine powder. Move to a huge bowl.

Add buckwheat, salt, cornstarch and cocoa and blend well. Gradually add the coconut oil and focus on the combination between your fingers until the flour and oil has completely consolidated. Add maple syrup and blend in with a wooden spoon until the mixture begins to meet up. Cover freely with cling wrap and pass on the mixture to rest for 10 minutes.

Once the batter has rested, equally partitioned it into four and press into every ramekin so the outside equitably covers the base and the sides. Prepare in the broiler, on the center rack, for 15 minutes. Eliminate from the stove and cool down as the filling can't be added when the outside layer is still hot. FOR THE FILLING:

DIRECTIONS

Heat oil in an enormous wok over medium-high hotness. Add onions and saute for 2-3 minutes until delicate, then, at that point, add ginger and garlic and cook for a further minute.

Add frozen vegetables and cook until thawed out and warmed all through, around 3-4 minutes. Mix in mushrooms and saute while oftentimes stirring.

Add turmeric and blend well to join, then, at that point, toss in cool rice and mix continually to fuse all fixings and separate any bunches. Pour in soy sauce. Serve immediately.

JAPANESE TEMPURA

Tempura is a Japanese dish consisting of either seafood or vegetables which have been battered in a very light and crisp coating. Our appetising vegan version uses sparkling water to ensure the batter stays light and crisp.

INGREDIENTS

DIRECTIONS

Heat the oil in an enormous pot or wok until it arrives at 350°c. Make sure every one of the vegetables are prepared and the oil is hot before you make the batter.

Whisk together the flour, cornstarch and salt then add the carbonated water and whisk until just combined then add the ice cubes. The way to making incredible tempura is to not over whisk the hitter, it is fine in the event that irregularities remain. You ought to likewise work quick and utilize the hitter promptly to guarantee it remains cold.

Dip the vegetables into the batter, one at a time, then carefully drop them into the oil. Try not to sear such a large number of immediately as this will lessen the temperature of the oil bringing about your tempura not getting firm. Cook each piece for 1-2 minutes, going once to guarantee they are equally cooked.

Remove with an opened spoon and move to a paper towel lined plate. Serve promptly once all the tempura have cooked.

TOD MAN KHAO POD (THAI CORN FRITTERS) (THAI CORN FRITTERS)

These wastes are stove prepared rather than singed, making them a lot better yet as yet holding the fresh and crunchy external covering. There are not very many advances engaged with this formula and it just requires 10 minutes to prepare.

INGREDIENTS

DIRECTIONS

Place tofu in a food processor or blender and heartbeat until it has become smooth. Remove the item from circulation. Preheat the stove to 170°c. Oil a baking plate with a little oil or line with material paper.

In a huge bowl consolidate pounded tofu, corn, flour, cornstarch, baking powder, scallions, cilantro, lime zing, soy sauce, red curry glue, bean stew drops and water. Blend well until a thick hitter has framed and all fixings are completely blended together.

Use an enormous spoon or frozen yogurt scoop to shape player into a round shape and straighten a little with your hands or utilizing the rear of a spoon to frame a fritter.

Place on the baking plate and rehash with remaining batter.

Bake for 27-30 minutes until edges have seared. Flip squander over following 15 minutes of cooking.

Serve promptly while hot and crispy.

CRUNCHY ASIAN SALAD WITH SWEET SESAME VINAIGRETTE

This vibrant, colorful and delicious salad is an Asian twist on a classic recipe which replaces rice with quinoa. It's loaded with veggies and is bursting with flavor from the addition of the Asian Vinaigrette.

INGREDIENTS

DIRECTIONS

Bring 2 cups water to a moving bubble then, at that point, add quinoa. Diminish to a delicate stew and cook covered for 17-20 minutes or as indicated by bundle headings. When cooked eliminate from hotness and cushion up utilizing a fork.

In a huge serving bowl add all coleslaw fixings together and throw until well combined. To make the vinaigrette whisk all fixings together.

Sprinkle vinaigrette over salad and serve.

The plate of mixed greens will keep in an impermeable holder in the ice chest for 2 days.

CHILI GARLIC MUSHROOMS

This easy side dish combines exotic flavors with a spicy kick. Stir-frying enables the mushrooms to be cooked to perfection and makes this a quick and easy dish using ingredients you are likely to already have in your cupboard.

INGREDIENTS

DIRECTIONS

Heat oil in a griddle or wok over medium-high hotness. When hot add garlic and saute for 30 seconds. Add mushrooms, parsley, bean stew, lemon juice, sherry and soy sauce.

Stir-fry for 5-6 minutes until the mushrooms are cooked all through. Mix continually to keep the mushrooms from consuming. Assuming that the blend is adhering to the lower part of the container add a sprinkle of water.

Season with salt and pepper and serve quickly while hot.

SAUTÉED BROCCOLI WITH ASIAN GARLIC SAUCE

Fragrant garlic and firm broccoli make this dish a top pick for focus points and in cafés. You can undoubtedly reproduce this delicious conventional dish in your own kitchen and it won't take you more than 10 minutes.

INGREDIENTS

DIRECTIONS

In a little bowl whisk together garlic, ginger and soy sauce.

Heat oil in a wok or skillet over medium-high hotness and add broccoli. Pan sear for 3-4 minutes, blending continually to keep the florets from adhering to the lower part of the pan.

Reduce hotness to medium-low and pour in soy sauce and cornstarch combination, mixing admirably to cover the entirety of the broccoli. Continue to mix for around 3 minutes for the sauce to thicken. Taste and season with salt and pepper if required.

Remove from hotness and serve promptly while hot.

SOFT CHINESE BAO BUNS

A baozi (bao bun) is a cushioned steamed bun with a soy bean glue filling that is extremely famous in Asian cooking. The bun is fragile and light with a flavorful focus, that can be eaten as a tidbit or filled in as a side dish to go with a fundamental meal.

INGREDIENTS

DIRECTIONS

In a little bowl add warm water (assuming you have a cooking thermometer the water should be 35°c) and delicately mix in the yeast. Put away for 5 minutes. You should see little air pockets framing at the surface.

In a huge bowl add the flour then, at that point, gradually pour in the water-yeast mixture, blending with a wooden spoon.

On a clean, daintily floured surface manipulate the batter with your hands for 5-6 minutes. It very well might be somewhat tacky from the outset however keep on tidying the surface with a little flour at a time and it should begin meeting up. Place in a huge bowl, cover with a fabric and pass on to rest in a dry region for 1 hour or until the batter pairs in size. After an hour move to a gently floured surface again and punch the air out by driving your clench hand into the focal point of the mixture, pulling it back into a ball shape and rehashing a couple times.

Roll the batter out into a long log of around 1-inch in width and utilizing a blade cut the sign into little bits of around 1-inch long. Straighten these with your hands or by squeezing them with the rear of a cup to shape a dainty round 'coin'. These are called baozi and are to be utilized as coverings. Remember they should be adequately huge to load up with stuffing. Put away in a solitary layer on an enormous plate or your kitchen work surface while you set up the filling.

Heat oil in a wok or dish over medium-high hotness, and when hot add ginger, garlic and bean glue, mixing continually for 1 moment until fragrant.

Add tofu, salt, and soy sauce and blend well. Pan sear for a further 5-7 minutes until the tofu is cooked. Add scallions then, at that point, eliminate from the heat.

Prepare your steamer.

Place one loaded tablespoon of the filling into the focal point of the baozi and start to crease the edges clockwise, squeezing the covering as you come. Move your thumb and pointer around in a clockwise bearing, squeezing the covering together until the bun is sealed.

Lightly brush the bun with a few oil on the top and base and spot in the liner. Rehash with residual coverings and filling.

Steam buns for 15 minutes. Serve quickly while warm.

COCONUT & LIME RICE

Coriander, coconut, and lime transform plain rice into a delicately flavored and exotic side dish, perfect to accompany a curry or main meal.

DIRECTIONS FOR INSTRUCTIONS ON HOW TO COOK WITH THESE INGREDIENTS

In a large saucepan bring salt, pepper, coconut milk and water to a boil then add the rice. Stir to combine and release any grains that have stuck to the bottom of the saucepan then reduce heat to a low simmer and cook covered for 14-17 minutes.

Remove from the hotness and mix in lime zing, lime juice and cilantro. Utilize a fork to cushion the rice up.

Serve quickly while channeling hot.

COCONUT CRUSTED TOFU BITES WITH CREAMY THAI GREEN SAUCE

This tasty bite-sized finger food can be served as an appetizer or as a side dish. The sweet crusty coating is made with shredded coconut and cashew nuts, and the bites are then dipped into a beautifully creamy and exotically flavored sauce.

INGREDIENTS

DIRECTIONS

To begin, remove the tofu from the bundling and press it between two towels to absorb excess liquid. You can utilize something weighted, like an enormous pot or slashing board and put this on top of the tofu to press out however much dampness as could reasonably be expected for at least 10 minutes. The tofu will retain a lot more flavor after this cycle. Following 10 minutes slash tofu into little scaled down cubes.

FOR THE DIPPING SAUCE:

While the tofu is being squeezed make the sauce. In a little pan consolidate coconut milk, green curry glue, pineapple juice, earthy colored sugar, and lime zing over medium-low hotness. When the fluid begins to stew eliminate 2 tbsp and\smove into a little bowl. Race in cornstarch or arrowroot powder until a smooth glue is shaped then empty once again into coconut milk coconut milk 7 minutes.

Remove from the hotness, move to a little serving bowl and permit to cool to room temperature. This sauce can be made as long as one day ahead, shrouded in saran wrap and left in the refrigerator overnight.

FOR THE COCONUT TOFU BITES:

Preheat the broiler to 190°c. Line a baking plate with material paper and shower with nonstick splash or oil with a little coconut oil.

In a medium bowl whisk mustard, coconut milk, lime, sugar, and salt until all around consolidated. Place cubed tofu in the combination and utilize a spatula to guarantee each piece is\s

covered. Pass on to absorb the flavor for at least 10 minutes.

In a shallow dish or enormous plate pour in the parched coconut and cashew nuts and blend well. Dunk every tofu piece into the coconutcashew blend and roll around to uniformly cover each side. Make a point to permit any overabundance coconut-mustard blend to trickle off prior to covering to keep the parched coconut from turning into a tacky mess.

Place every coconut crusted piece on the baking plate and rehash with outstanding tofu. Heat for 25-30 minutes, turning once following 15 minutes, until brilliant brown. Serve right away or permit to cool to room temperature.

DESSERTS COCONUT MATCHA TARTS

Finally, a pastry that is sound! The outside layer is produced using oats, coconut, and buckwheat flour, and the smooth and rich filling highlights crude cashew nuts, coconut cream, and very solid matcha. The expansion of matcha powder gives the filling a brilliantly lively green color.

INGREDIENTS

* FOR THE COCONUT CREAM: This should either be the assortment you can purchase in a hard square or you can take a container of full-fat coconut milk, place it in the cooler short-term and utilize the hard cream that will have framed at the top.

DIRECTIONS

FOR THE CRUST:

Preheat the stove to 350° F. Line the foundation of 4 ramekins (around 4.5 inches in\sdistance across) with material paper and oil the edges with around 1 teaspoon of coconut oil and set aside.

Place oats and coconut in a food processor or fast blender and heartbeat until it turns into a fine powder. Move to a huge bowl.

Add buckwheat, salt, cornstarch and cocoa and blend well. Gradually add the coconut oil and focus on the combination between your fingers until the flour and oil has completely consolidated. Add maple syrup and blend in with a wooden spoon until the mixture begins to meet up. Cover freely with cling wrap and pass on the mixture to rest for 10 minutes.

Once the batter has rested, equally partitioned it into four and press into every ramekin so the outside equitably covers the base and the sides. Prepare in the broiler, on the center rack, for 15 minutes. Eliminate from the stove and cool down as the filling can't be added when the outside layer is still hot. FOR THE FILLING:

Place the agar flakes in a small saucepan with ½ cup of water and bring to a boil then lower to a simmer. Stew for 15 minutes, blending regularly, until the chips have disintegrated however much as could reasonably be expected. Eliminate from the hotness and permit to chill off for 5 minutes or so.

While the agar agar is cooling down place drained cashews, coconut cream, matcha, maple syrup, and vanilla into a blender and pulse until smooth, scraping down the sides a few times, then add the agar agar and pulse again a few times until the mixture is completely smooth. Add the dried up coconut and heartbeat more than once to join it into the mixture.

Evenly empty the filling into the four ramekins and smooth over the top with the rear of a spoon. Set the tart to the side to set for 30-40 minutes then serve.

DWI JIAN (FRIED SESAME BALLS)

These sweet fried balls are commonly served as Dim Sum and are made of a soft rice flour dough that is filled with red bean paste, then covered in sesame seeds and deep fried to crisp perfection. You'll be amazed at how simple it is to make this trustworthy recipe in your own kitchen!

INGREDIENTS

DIRECTIONS

Rice flour, sugar, and salt are mixed together in a medium bowl. Blend in the bubbling water until the mixture is unpleasant, then add the vegetable oil.

Transfer to a kitchen surface that has been lightly dusted with glutinous rice flour and work for a few minutes, or until the oil has completely absorbed.

Cut the batter into 8 equal pieces after rolling it out into a slim 'log.' Carry each ball out into a "circle," then spoon 1 to 2 teaspoons of red bean glue into the center. Seal completely to prevent red bean paste from leaking out, then shape into a round ball.

In a wok over medium heat, heat the vegetable oil. It should stretch between 210 and 250 degrees Celsius. Prepare two dishes: one with sesame seeds and the other with water. To ensure that the sesame seeds stick, quickly dip each ball into the water to lightly coat it, then dip it in the sesame seeds and gently roll it between your palms. Continuing with the remaining balls is a good idea.

Place the balls carefully into the hot oil (you may need to do this in batches to avoid overcrowding the container) and fry for 5 minutes without touching or moving them, as the sesame seeds may fall off. Turn the balls over with a metal tong after 5 minutes.

The balls will float to the oil's surface after initially remaining at the bottom of the pan. When they start to float, use metal utensils or a couple of chopsticks to gently lower the balls into the hot oil. Once you start squeezing the balls against the sides, you'll notice that they grow in size. To guarantee a round shape, try pressing each ball uniformly on each side. When the balls have grown to multiple times their original size and have begun to cook, remove them from the heat with an open spoon and place them on a paper towel lined plate.

Allow to cool slightly before serving. Sesame balls should be consumed the same day they are prepared because they do not keep well the next day.

RICE WITH MANGO AND COCONUT STICKY

Make a straightforward and easy-to-plan adaptation of a true Thai dish. Smooth and thick rice is softly seasoned with sweet coconut and topped off with fresh mangos. This is a generous pastry that is sure to please the entire crowd.

INGREDIENTS

Once the sticky rice has been saturated, drain the excess moisture by spreading it out on a large fabric or towel and wiping it off.

Steam for 15 minutes after placing the rice in a liner.

While the rice is steaming hot, combine the coconut milk, sugar, and salt in a small pan. Maintain a low heat and avoid allowing it to bubble. When the sugar has broken up and the milk has thickened a little, approximately 5-6 minutes, remove from the hotness. 12 cup milk should be saved in a small bowl. Continue steaming for another 10-15 minutes after pouring 12 cups of coconut milk over the sticky rice.

Remove the rice from the liner and place it on a serving plate or bowl after it has finished cooking. Allow 10 minutes for the rice to cool before pouring the remaining 12 cup coconut milk over it and arranging the mango solid shapes on top.

Serve immediately, garnished with broiled dark sesame seeds if desired.

SESAME SEEDS ON CRISPY BANANA FRITTERS

The fresh and crunchy brilliant player on the outside contrasts with the sweet and delicate banana on the inside. The temperature of the oil must be precisely controlled to finish these wastes. If the oil isn't hot enough when they're frying, they'll turn greasy and soggy.

In a large skillet or wok (11 2 inches), heat the oil until it is extremely hot. If you have a cooking thermometer, heat the oil to 180°C. Place a small slice of bread in the oil and wait 30 seconds.

While the oil heats up, combine the parched coconut, two flours, sesame seeds, salt, sugar, and water with a mixer until a smooth and thick batter forms.

Dip each banana piece in the player to evenly coat it, then place it in the hot oil with caution. Fry the wastes in batches for 3-4 minutes, or until golden brown, taking care not to overcrowd the pan.

Remove every banana squander with an opened spoon and place on a kitchen towel-lined plate. Replace the battered banana pieces with new ones that haven't been battered yet. Dust

serve immediately while still hot, dusted with icing sugar

HUP TUL WOO (CHINESE SWEET WALNUT SOUP) For a long time, the Chinese have adored this rich and velvety pastry. It uses pecans, rice, and coconut milk to create a dish that falls somewhere between porridge and rice pudding. It's usually served hot, which makes it incredibly soothing.

DIRECTIONS

Fill a bowl halfway with water and add the rice. Allow for 2 12 hours of rice splashing by covering the bowl with a plate or saran wrap. Preheat the oven to 350 degrees Fahrenheit and preheat the broiler.

Arrange pecans in a single layer on a baking sheet lined with parchment paper. Cook for 10-12 minutes, or until fragrant and sautéed. Remove from the heat and set aside for 5 minutes to cool.

Fill a food processor with the rice, pecans, and 4 cups of water after draining the rice. After that, transfer to a saucepan and beat until smooth. Heat the rice-pecan mixture on a low heat setting, then add the sugar and salt. 15 minutes of stewing

Using a sifter, strain the mixture into a separate pot and add the coconut milk. Heat for 5 minutes, then spoon into 4 bowls, finishing with a couple of walnuts in each.

RICE PUDDING WITH GINGER INFLATION IN JAPANESE

This Japanese-inspired formula is luscious and smooth, with a delicate ginger flavor that's not overpowering. Short grain rice is recommended for engrossing the flavorful milk and creating a satiny texture.

DIRECTIONS

Water, white sugar, and earthy colored sugar are heated in a small pot over medium-low heat. Bring to a boil, then reduce the heat to a low stew temperature. Cook, stirring occasionally, for 25 minutes with the syrup.

In the meantime, wrap the ginger in cheesecloth and secure it with a piece of string. Combine almond milk, soy milk, and ginger in a saucepan over low heat. Cook for around 20 minutes, stirring occasionally, to achieve a delicate stew.

Take out the ginger pack and throw it away. Bring the mixture to a boil, then add the rice and syrup.

Reduce heat to medium and cook for 30 minutes, uncovered, until the pudding thickens and the rice is tender.

Remove from the heat and top with cut strawberries and solidified ginger in bowls.

ICE CREAM WITH BLACK SESEME SEEDS

Black sesame seeds are well-known in Asia and are associated with a variety of delectable dishes. Their magnificently nutty flavor and magnificent dark tone are used in a sweet frozen yogurt dessert in this extraordinary formula. This velvety, rich, and delectable frozen yogurt is made without the use of a frozen yogurt maker.

INGREDIENTS

DIRECTIONS

In a dry skillet, toast the dark sesame seeds over medium heat until fragrant and popping. Remove from the heat and set aside to cool for a few minutes in a small bowl. Fill a food processor, high-powered blender, or espresso machine halfway with the seeds and process until they're finely ground. To make a thick paste, transfer to a small bowl and combine with maple syrup.

Pour 1 container of coconut milk, sugar, and salt into a pan set over medium heat and whisk until the sugar has dissolved.

Pour the dairy-free milk into a medium mixing bowl, then whisk in the cornflour until completely smooth with no knots. Add this mixture to the coconut milk and increase the heat to medium high, whisking constantly to ensure no lumps form for about 5 minutes or until the mixture thickens.

Remove from the heat, transfer to a large mixing bowl, and stir in the sesame seed glue and vanilla pith until everything is thoroughly combined. To prevent a skin from framing, wrap it in cling wrap and place it in the refrigerator for at least 2 hours to chill.

Using a frozen yogurt maker, churn the mixture as directed by the machine. If you don't have a frozen yogurt maker, pour the mixture into a level metal plate, cover, and place in the refrigerator to chill. After 40 minutes, give the mixture a good fork crush to separate the ice precious stones, and repeat this process two more times after each brief interval. If you want your frozen yogurt to be completely smooth, instead of pounding it with a fork, you could blend it in a food processor.

Remove the frozen yogurt from the freezer 15 minutes before serving to allow it to soften a bit. In a tightly sealed freezer holder, frozen yogurt will keep for a long time.

COCONUT ICE CREAM WITH WATERMELON

This sugar-free frozen yogurt takes only 10 minutes to prepare. It's energizing and light, and it's a great way to keep a sweet tooth in check.

INGREDIENTS

DIRECTIONS

Set aside a cling wrap-lined bread pan or cake skillet. In a blender, combine all of the ingredients and pulse until completely smooth.

Fill a fixed tin halfway with the mixture and cover loosely with saran wrap; freeze for 3 hours.

Remove from the tin after 3 hours and set aside to defrost at room temperature for 10 minutes.

Using a blade, break up the cream into smaller chunks and re-blend it. To achieve a smooth and rich surface, it should be re-mixed. Return to the lined tin and pulse for another 2-3 minutes.

Place in the freezer for 30 minutes before serving. Frozen yogurt can be kept in the refrigerator for up to three months if wrapped in saran wrap.

COCONUT PANCAKES IN THAI STYLE

These delectable little hotcakes are a popular Thai street food that will transport you to a tropical paradise of coconuts. They're light and feathery, with a firm brilliant coating, so they're not too heavy after a big meal.

INGREDIENTS

DIRECTIONS

In a large mixing bowl, combine all of the ingredients and whisk until smooth. If the hitter appears to be too dry, add 1 tablespoon of water at a time.

In a medium-high-heat skillet, heat the vegetable oil. Once the oil is hot, make fritters in small batches by spooning 1 heaped tbsp of batter into the pan, flattening slightly with a spatula by gently pressing down to form the shape of a fritter, and frying for 2-3 minutes on one side, then flipping and cooking for another 2-3 minutes until golden brown and crispy.

While you fry the remaining fritters, remove them to a paper towel lined plate. Serve as soon as possible, while the food is still hot and crisp.

DIPPING SAUCE WITH SWEET CHILI

This sauce's versatility allows it to be used in a variety of applications. If you're short on time, drizzle the sauce over noodles for a quick and easy dinner, or drizzle it over spring rolls, sesame crackers, or fries for a flavor boost.

INGREDIENTS

DIRECTIONS

In a mixing bowl, combine all of the fixings and beat on high until well combined and the sugar is dissolved. Refrigerate for 5-7 days in an airtight container.

OYSTER SAUCE WITHOUT THE ANIMAL

Oyster sauce is a common ingredient in stir fries, dips, and soups, and is a must-have in any Asian kitchen. This vegan version mimics the umami flavor of oyster sauce with miso paste, making it a great vegan substitute.

INGREDIENTS

DIRECTIONS

In a pot, bring 1 cup of water to a boil, then add the stock 3D square and miso and stir until the miso is completely dissolved. Reduce the heat to a lively stew, then add the cornflourwater mixture and stir well until it thickens.

Cook, stirring constantly, until the maple syrup and soy sauce have thickened.

Transfer to a container and remove from the heat. Allow the clam sauce to cool to room temperature before refrigerating it fixed for up to 2 weeks.

SAUCE WITH PEANUTS IN IT

Peanut satay is a delicious dipping sauce, salad dressing, or tofu marinade. It's quick and simple to make, and you can make it with pantry staples.

INGREDIENTS

DIRECTIONS

Combine all fixings aside from the sesame seeds, and hotness in a pot over medium-low. Heat until fixings have dissolved together and become smooth and velvety yet don't bring to a boil.

Once cooked, eliminate from hotness and add sesame seeds. Pour over noodles or use as a dunking sauce.

Store in the ice chest in a sealed shut compartment for up to 5 days.

SPINACH AND SESAME CRACKERS

The spinach in this formula is accustomed to carry a dynamic green tone to these wafers without overwhelming the flavor. The saltines have a sweet nutty taste, on account of the sesame seeds and are wonderful when plunged in sweet stew sauce or nut satay sauce.

INGREDIENTS

DIRECTIONS

Preheat the broiler to 200°C. Line a baking plate with material paper. Add spinach to a blender or food processor with ¼ cup water and heartbeat until totally smooth. Remove the item from circulation.

In an enormous bowl add flour, baking powder, salt, pepper and sesame seeds and blend to join. Mix in the spinach-water combination alongside sesame oil and manipulate with your hands until you have framed a smooth batter. Add somewhat more flour assuming that the mixture is excessively tacky, or a tablespoon more water assuming that it appears to dry.

On a clean and delicately floured surface carry the batter out into a slight long rectangular shape. Cut into equally measured scaled down squares (going across and down - length and width shrewd) utilizing a sharp blade or pizza shaper. Move to the baking tray.

Bake for 20 minutes or until the edges have browned.

Store in a sealed shut holder at room temperature for up to 1 week.

EDAMAME PÂTÉ

An earthy and fresh pâté made with edamame, mint, and lime juice. Perfect as a spread for crackers and wraps, or you could even add a little water and use it as a dip for sushi or chips.

INGREDIENTS

DIRECTIONS

Place edamame in a pot, pour in sufficient water to completely lower them then, at that point, heat to the point of boiling. Diminish and stew for 5 minutes until they are delicate. Channel well and move to a food processor.

Add any remaining fixings to the food processor and mix until you have a smooth paste. Keep in a hermetically sealed holder for 3-4 days.

THAI MANGO-COCONUT BUBBLE TEA

Bubble tea, otherwise called pearl milk tea, is a Taiwanese beverage that has acquired fame throughout the most recent couple of years. Custard pearls can be found in any Asian shop or the global part of an enormous general store. This interestingly enhanced sweet tea is exceptionally simple to make at home and you can explore different avenues regarding different flavors.

INGREDIENTS

DIRECTIONS

Make 2-3 cups of solid tea. Place the pot of tea in the fridge to cool and soak for around 15-20 minutes.

In a little pan heat 2 cups of water to the point of boiling. Add 1 tbsp sugar and custard pearls, diminish to a low stew and cook for 15 minutes or as per bundle bearings. Channel water, move pearls to a little bowl and refrigerate for 20-30 minutes or until chilled.

In a mixed drink shaker pour in tea, coconut milk, maple syrup and ice and shake energetically briefly or two.

Place custard pearls and mango in a glass and pour over coconut milk combinatio\sn. Serve cold.

CPSIA information can be obtained
at www.ICGtesting.com
Printed in the USA
LVHW050601140422
716000LV00007B/356